Learning to Listen

Developing students' ability to listen actively for sustained amounts of time

Tania Mills

Dip. Tchg, Higher Dip/Tchg

Curriculum Concepts

comprehensive coverage

Learning to Listen

ISBN 9781906125462

Ordering Code – UK0328

Curriculum Concepts UK

The Old School

Upper High Street

Bedlinog

Mid-Glamorgan CF46 6SA

Email: orders@curriculumconcepts.co.uk

www.curriculumconcepts.co.uk

Contents

Introduction

Listening skills are essential if students are to succeed in all areas of the curriculum, and in their every-day lives.

This resource will provide continuous opportunities for students to develop good listening skills in the classroom and build their ability to listen actively for a sustained period of time.

Curriculum Links

The National Curriculum states quite clearly what students should be taught to do under the listening strand. It says that listening, speaking, reading and writing should be integrated. However within this there is a place to 'teach' listening as an isolated specific skill as well, just as we teach handwriting as a specific skill that then flows through to students writing stories with fluency. Alongside specific skill teaching there should be opportunities to practice what they have learned in an integrated way.

Listening – Key Stage 1

Knowledge, skills and understanding

2. To listen, understand and respond to others, pupils should be taught to:
   a) sustain concentration
   b) remember specific points that interest them
   c) make relevant comments
   d) listen to others' reactions
   e) ask questions to clarify their understanding
   f) identify and respond to sound patterns in language

Listening – Key Stage 2

2. To listen, understand and respond appropriately to other, pupils should be taught to:
   a) identify the gist of an account or key points in a discussion and evaluate what they hear
   b) ask relevant questions to clarify, extend and follow up ideas
   c) recall and re-present important features of an argument, talk, reading, radio or television programme, film
   d) identify features of language used for a specific purpose (for example, to persuade, instruct or entertain)
   e) respond to others appropriately, taking into account what they say

How to use this resource

The story should be READ ALOUD by the teacher. (The students do not read the story themselves.) Pre-read the story to familiarize yourself with the content. As you read it to the students, try to use a calm soothing voice, and avoid speaking too quickly. Pause at the end of each sentence, and at the end of paragraphs to let the information 'sink in'.

Each story has two activity sheets to accompany it.

1. Listening comprehension activities directly related to the information in the story and
2. Creative Expression activities which develop the content of the stories in creative ways.

When students first start using this resource, they may find it difficult to concentrate for the entire time. This is a skill which they will develop as you continue to use the resource. Insist that students are quiet, or they will interrupt other students' thought processes. It is also ideal if the students keep their eyes closed, as this will help them retain the information by limiting distractions. Explain to students the purpose of the activities and talk about what it means to 'listen actively' and 'for a sustained period of time'.

Suggested lesson format and extention ideas

1. A CALMING EXPERIENCE

The students lie (or sit) quietly, and listen. The teacher reads the piece at the top of each story to set the scene. It is important to say this the same each time so that students get into a routine. The words set the scene for them and get them tuned into listening.

The teacher slowly reads out the story. It is useful to relax students after a busy lunch hour, or if the students are particularly unsettled for some reason. You may also find that students will ask you repeat a favourite story.

2. INTRODUCING THE ACTIVITY GRADUALLY

i) Look at the Listening Comprehension sheet for the information they will need and cue students to listen for particular information before you start reading.

ii) At first write these cues on the board and then move to giving them orally.

iii) At first let the students make notes as they hear the information come up in the story and progress to them remembering/retaining the information until the end of the story.

iv) Once the students are at a point where you give them the cues orally and they remember them without writing them down, reduce the number of cues you give until you reach the point where you give no cues before reading the story at all.

3. LISTENING COMPREHENSION ACTIVITY SHEETS*

After the story has been read to them, the students complete the Listening Comprehension sheet. This can be done in silence, and may be retained by the teacher to gather information for assessment. (Answers are on page 61.) Another way for the Listening Comprehension sheet to be used is to discuss the worksheet as a class or groups, and allow the students to complete it in a more informal way. This method is another way the activity can be introduced to students. Begin by doing it as a group activity and once students understand what is required begin to do it as an individual exercise. When completed as a group exercise it gives an opportunity for inter personal listening and speaking practise as the students discuss the answers and come to a consensus almost themselves.

4. CREATIVE EXPRESSION ACTIVITY SHEETS*

This may be used instead of, or in conjunction with the Listening Comprehension sheet. It is also ideal as an independent activity for fast workers. This sheet may be used as an assessment tool to gather information on the child's ability to be creative and to follow instructions.

5. DRAMATIC EXPRESSION

The students listen to the story as the teacher reads it. As the teacher reads the story for a second time, the students use drama to act out the story. Another option could be for the teacher to record the story onto a tape and replay it, so she/he may join in and provide a model.

*   The activity sheets may not be appropriate for younger students who are unable to read or write yet. However, you are still able to use the stories. Follow up the reading with a shared writing activity with the whole class, or encourage students to record their ideas in the form of drama or pictures.

A Visit To The Fire Station

Hello children. It's time for our Learning To Listen story.
Lie down with your back on the mat or lean forward and put your head on your table. Make sure you're not touching anyone. Close your eyes. Remember we are learning to actively listen for a sustained amount of time.
Now take a deep breath, hold it, and let it out slowly. Do it again, breathe in ... and out. Breathe in, and out. I want you to keep taking deep breaths while I read you a story.

Listen carefully.

Today we are going to visit the fire station. When you arrive at the station, you knock on the door. You wait for a moment, and then you hear footsteps coming. When the door opens, there is a man standing there with a big smile on his face. But he is not wearing a red jacket, red pants, big black boots, or a yellow helmet. He is wearing shorts and a t-shirt.

He holds his hand out for you to shake. "Welcome to the fire-station," he says. "My name is Fire fighter Sam. I am going to show you around."

You shake your head. "How can you be a fire fighter?" you ask. "You're not wearing your jacket, pants, black boots, and helmet!"

Fireman Sam laughs. "I don't wear my fire-fighting gear when I'm in the station! It would get very hot. Come inside and I'll show you where we keep the gear."

You follow Sam into the station. He leads you down a long corridor. Sam points as you walk past some open doors. "That is the kitchen where we cook our meals. These are the bedrooms where we sleep. That is the gymnasium where we exercise. That is the room where we read books and watch television. This is the bathroom and showers where we get clean again after we've been to a fire."

You're wondering where the fire engine is, when Fire fighter Sam stops walking. He turns around and looks at you. "Listen carefully," he says. "If you hear the bells ring, it means that there is a fire, and the fire fighters have to go and put it out. You must stay out of the way so we can get away quickly. Do you understand?"

You nod your head. Then Sam says, "Come and see the fire engine." You follow him through a door, and there it is! It's huge and **red**! (Change to appropriate colour)

"Come on up," says Fire fighter Sam. He climbs up into the cab and reaches a hand down to pull you up. Up you go! And then you're sitting in the driver's seat of a fire engine! It's a long way up! Sam shows you the special radio that the fire fighters use to find out how to get to the fire. He also shows you the button to push to make the siren and the lights go on. Then you see helmets sitting beside each seat. Fire fighter Sam lets you try one on. It's very big and heavy on your head! It has a visor to pull down that protects your eyes. When you take it off, it feels very heavy in your hands.

"Come and have a look," says Sam. You look over, and see a great big pair of black boots. There are pants attached to them. "When fire fighters go to a fire, they just have to jump in the engine and put their feet into the boots," says Sam. "They pull up the pants, and they put on their jackets."

Wow! They must have to get dressed very quickly. Sam helps you out of the cab. You walk around the engine, looking at all the hoses and ladders. There are also hammers and torches and first aid gear. Suddenly, there is loud noise! The emergency bells are ringing! Quickly you move back out of the way, just like Sam told you. All of the other fire fighters come running out of the station. They jump into the engine, the siren starts up, and the lights start flashing. Then they're off, to help someone in trouble.

"Thank you for coming!" yells Fireman Sam as the engine races away. "See you next time!"

We're going to take three deep breaths again. Breathe in, hold, and slowly breathe out. Then again, breathe in, and out. Breathe in, and out.
Good. Now slowly sit up.
We've finished.
Well done.

A Visit To The Fire Station

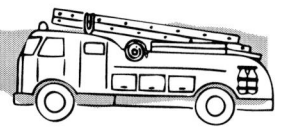

Listening Comprehension

1. Put a circle around the special gear that a fire fighter wears to fight fires. Colour them in.

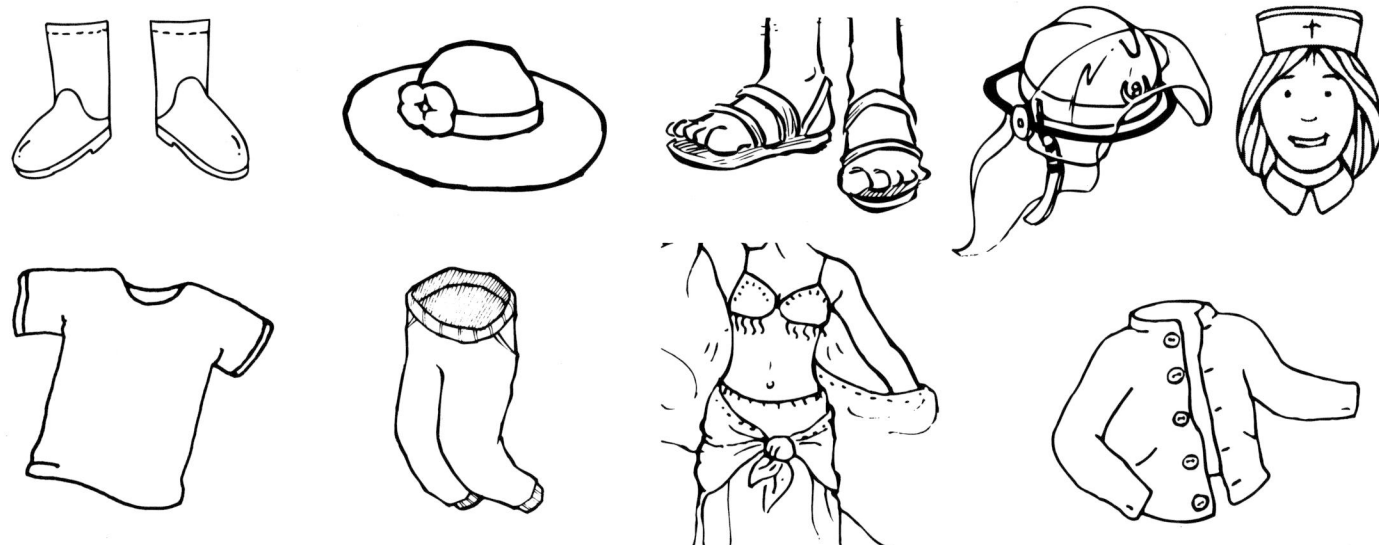

2. Here are some statements about the story. Are they true or false? Put a circle around the correct answer.

a) Fireman Sam opens the door in his uniform.	True	False
b) In the station there is a kitchen.	True	False
c) If the bells ring, you must stay out of the way.	True	False
d) You are not allowed to try on the helmet.	True	False
e) The fire engine has ladders and hoses on it.	True	False
f) The fire fighters wear red boots.	True	False

3. Draw a picture of the fire engine in the story.

Creative Expression

1. Where do you think the fire fighters were going? Write a story about them.

   ....
   ....
   ....
   ....
   ....
   ....
   ....

2. Draw plan of the fire station. Include the kitchen, the bedrooms, the gymnasium, the lounge, the bathroom and the fire engine bay.

3. Would you like to be a fire fighter? Write some sentences about it.

   ....
   ....
   ....
   ....
   ....
   ....

Dinosaur Dig

Hello children. It's time for our Learning To Listen story.
Lie down with your back on the mat or lean forward and put your head on your table. Make sure you're not touching anyone. Close your eyes. Remember we are learning to actively listen for a sustained amount of time.
Now take a deep breath, hold it, and let it out slowly. Do it again, breathe in ... and out. Breathe in, and out. I want you to keep taking deep breaths while I read you a story.

Listen carefully.

Today you are going to look for dinosaur fossils. You have a map, with the place you think the bones are hidden marked on it. You also have a backpack, and inside it are a torch, a small pick, a small brush and a large piece of cloth.

You read the instructions on the map. They say, "Follow the track into the forest. Stop when you come to the big tree in the clearing." You can see the track from the side of the road, so you follow it.

As you walk you notice that the trees seem to be getting bigger and bigger. Suddenly you come to a large clearing, and in the centre is the most enormous tree you have ever seen. You walk over and stretch your arms out. It would take ten people of your size to stand in a ring around it! You step back and look at your map again. It says, "Turn to the right, and walk forward into the forest 30 paces." You turn to the right, and walk forward 30 paces. There is no track here, and it is hard to walk. You have to climb over and under the huge logs that have fallen in your way. Finally you have walked the 30 paces. You look at the map again. It says, "Look down and look for the dinosaur fossils here". You look down. At first you can't see anything, so you kneel down and look closely at the ground. It's quite dark down here so you get your torch out of your backpack. You switch it on and a beam of light shines onto the forest floor. Now you can see them! There are fossils on a muddy bank that runs along in front of you!

You take the small pick and the small brush from your backpack. Then you carefully start to dig away the dirt with your pick. The dirt is quite soft and it crumbles away easily. You're being very careful because you don't want to damage the fossils. Now you can see them better! The one that you can see is big and white. You take your small brush, and use it to brush the dirt away. You keep working away carefully, using the small pick to move the dirt away, and the small brush to clean it. Pick, pick, pick. Brush, brush, brush. Soon you have nearly moved all the dirt away. The fossil is ready to come out! Very carefully, you move the last of the dirt away. Then you slowly lift the fossil down onto the forest floor. You look at it in wonder. You think it is a dinosaur bone! It looks like the leg bone of an Oviraptor! The rest of the dinosaur's skeleton must be here as well, but you'll need a lot more people to help you get them out. For now, you're just going to take this fossil back to show everyone.

You take the cloth from your backpack, and carefully wrap it around the fossil. Then you put it into your backpack, and put the backpack on your back. You note down on the map the exact place that you found the dinosaur bones. Now it's time to go. Thirty paces back, over and under the fallen logs. When you reach the enormous tree, you turn left, and take the track back to the road.

You just can't wait to get back and show everyone what you have found. And you also can't wait to go back and find the rest of the dinosaur! What exciting work!

We're going to take three deep breaths again. Breathe in, hold, and slowly breathe out. Then again, breathe in, and out. Breathe in, and out.
Good. Now slowly sit up.
We've finished.
Well done.

Dinosaur Dig

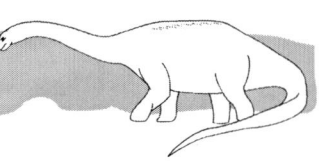

Listening Comprehension

1. Here are some sentences from the story. Some of the information is not correct. Put a circle around True or False.

a) You have a torch in your backpack.	True False
b) The tree in the clearing is very small.	True False
c) You walk 30 paces into the forest.	True False
d) The fossil is easy to find.	True False
e) It is the leg bone of a Brontosaurus.	True False
f) You put the fossil in the cloth.	True False

2. Here are some questions about the story. Choose your answer from the list below.

an enormous tree	a torch	fallen logs
30 paces	a small brush	a cloth

a) What is in the middle of the clearing? ....

b) How many steps did you take into the forest? ....

c) What did you wrap the fossil in? ....

d) What did you climb over and under? ....

e) What did you use to clean the fossil? ....

f) What did you use to help you see? ....

3. Draw a map of your fossil-finding journey.

Start here

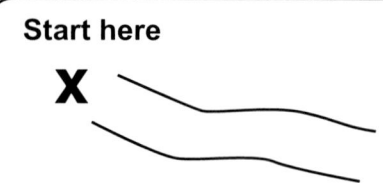

Dinosaur Dig

Creative Expression

1. You are in charge of organising a team of people to go and get the rest of the dinosaur bones. Make a list of all things you will need.

....

....

....

....

2. How would it feel to find some real dinosaur fossils? Which dinosaur would you like to find? Write a story about finding your own dinosaur.

....

....

....

....

....

....

....

....

....

....

3. Draw a picture of you on your own dinosaur dig.

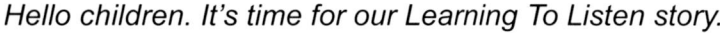

Hello children. It's time for our Learning To Listen story.
Lie down with your back on the mat or lean forward and put your head on your table.
Make sure you're not touching anyone. Close your eyes. Remember we are learning to actively listen for a sustained amount of time.
Now take a deep breath, hold it, and let it out slowly. Do it again, breathe in ... and out. Breathe in, and out. I want you to keep taking deep breaths while I read you a story.

Listen carefully.

Today you're going to the zoo. It's going to be so much fun, because you're going to help a zookeeper feed the animals!

You arrive there early in the morning. You knock at a door that says 'Keepers Entrance'. A woman opens the door. She is wearing a dark green shirt, and dark green shorts. She has thick wool socks on her feet, and heavy boots. Her long hair is in a plait, and she is wearing a wide-brimmed hat.

"Hello," she says with a smile. "I'm Keeper Jones. You're going to help me feed the animals this morning."

You follow Keeper Jones into a part of the zoo you have never seen before. "This is our kitchen," says Keeper Jones. You go into the building. All the food is in big plastic bins, one blue, one yellow, and one red. "Help me put these bins on the truck," says Keeper Jones.

You grab the bin closest to you. You put it up on the back of the truck. Once all the food is on the truck, you jump in beside Keeper Jones.

"The first animals we're going to feed are the sea lions," says Keeper Jones. You drive around to a huge swimming pool. As you get closer, the sea lions see the truck. They start to make loud 'arf, arf' noises! Keeper Jones stops the truck. You both jump out. She pulls out a blue bin and takes off the lid. In there are dozens of shiny fish! She opens a gate, and then carries the bin into the pool area. "Come and help me," she says. She picks up a fish by the tail, and throws it into the air. A big seal lion rushes out of the water and catches it in his mouth! You take a fish by the tail and throw it in too. Another sea lion catches it, and eats it in one gulp! You both keep throwing out the fish until they are gone!

You jump into the truck and drive away. "The second animals we're going to feed are the monkeys," says Keeper Jones. You drive towards a big enclosure full of swings and climbing frames. As you get closer, the monkeys see the trucks. They start to chatter and squawk! Keeper Jones stops the truck. You jump out and help her lift down the yellow bin. She opens a gate, and carries the bin into the enclosure. "Come and help me put out the food for the monkeys," she says. She opens the lid, and inside are all kinds of fruits, nuts and seeds. You help her put the food into trays all over the feeding area. Then once you're out of the enclosure, she opens a little door and the monkeys come rushing in! They grab the food and eat it!

"The third animal we are going to feed is the lion," says Keeper Jones. You drive towards a big enclosure with a high fence around it. You cannot see the lion. Keeper Jones stops the truck. "Stay here," she says. "It's not safe for you to help now." She carries the red bin into the enclosure. You watch as she opens the container and takes out some huge bones with lots of meat on them. She lays them out, and then she comes out, and opens a door. Out comes the lion! He's huge, and he's roaring! He rushes down and starts to drag the bones away to eat.

What a great sight! It has been so much fun feeding the animals. You would love to come back another day, and feed some different animals. Thank you, Keeper Jones!

We're going to ep breaths again. Breathe in, hold, and slowly breathe out. Then again, breathe in, and out. Breathe in, and out.
Good. Now slowly sit up.
We've finished.
Well done.

Feeding Time At The Zoo

Listening Comprehension

1. Draw a line to match the items from the story with the correct colour. Then colour them in.

a) ranger's shirt   red

b) bin of fish   green

c) ranger's shorts   yellow

d) bin of fruit, nuts and seeds   blue

e) bin of meat   green

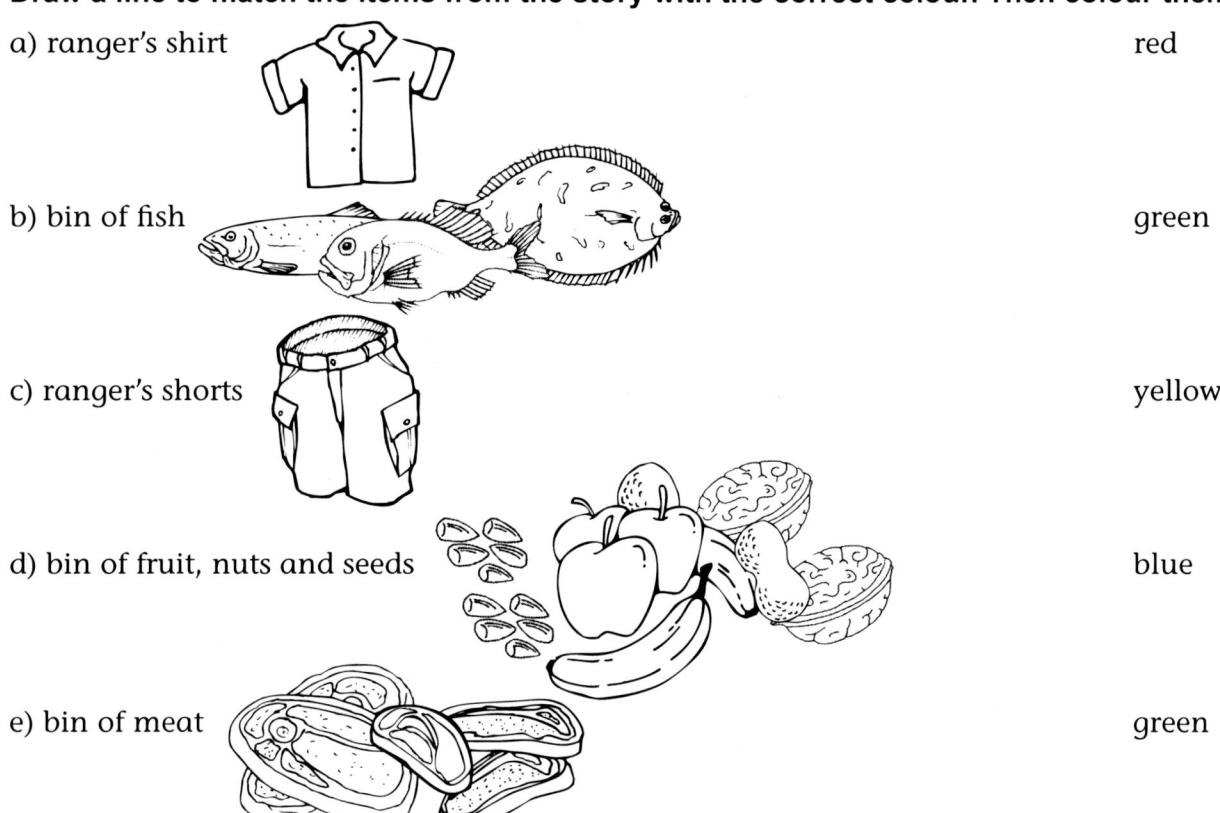

2. Here are some statements about the story. Are they True or False? Put a circle around the correct answer.

a) The sea lions like to eat fish.   True False
b) The monkeys like to eat bread.   True False
c) The lion was friendly.   True False
d) The lion liked to eat fruit.   True False
e) You would like to help another day.   True False

3. The three animals you fed lived in very different enclosures. Draw a picture of each of them.

the sea lion enclosure	the monkey enclosure	the lion enclosure

Feeding Time At The Zoo

Creative Expression

1. **Imagine you were the keeper at the zoo. Answer these questions.**

   What is your favourite animal? ....

   What does it eat? ....

   Write a story about feeding your favourite animal.

   ....

   ....

   ....

   ....

   ....

   ....

   ....

   ....

2. **What other jobs would you have if you were a keeper? Write a list of them.**

   ....

   ....

   ....

   ....

   ....

   ....

   ....

3. **Draw a picture of you doing your favourite keeper job.**

Hello children. It's time for our Learning To Listen story.
Lie down with your back on the mat or lean forward and put your head on your table.
Make sure you're not touching anyone. Close your eyes. Remember we are learning to actively listen for a sustained amount of time.
Now take a deep breath, hold it, and let it out slowly. Do it again, breathe in ... and out. Breathe in, and out. I want you to keep taking deep breaths while I read you a story.

Listen carefully.

Tonight is fireworks night. You can't wait for it to get dark so you can watch the fireworks show. It seems to take such a long time, but finally the sun goes down. You put on long pants, shoes, a jacket and a cap. It's time to go to see the fireworks!

When you get there you sit on one of the seats that have been put out for the audience. Everyone is waiting patiently for the fireworks to start. You're far away from the people who are lighting the fireworks, but you're pleased to see they have brought fire extinguishers with them!

Now the show is going to start! What will be first?

Suddenly, there is a huge bang! It is so loud that you jump out of your seat! Then you hear the whiz of a rocket in the sky, and then a loud pop as hundreds of tiny red stars explode above you! Then there is another bang, then a whiz, then a pop, as tiny green stars explode above you! Then there is another bang, then a whiz, then a pop, as tiny blue stars explode above you! Over and over it goes, red, green, blue. Red, green, blue. Finally the last star disappears. What a great display! What will come next?

Then you see one of the fireworks people lighting a firework on the ground. There is a loud fizzing noise, and then golden sparks come rushing out into the air! They go out in a wide curve, and then they fall down in a golden rain. It is so pretty to watch. After the golden rain has finished, then silver sparks come rushing out into the air! They go out in a wide curve, and then they fall down in a silvery rain. What a great display! What will come next?

Then you see another fireworks person lighting some fireworks. Suddenly sparks come flying out of a circle that is nailed to the fence. It's a Catherine Wheel! Round it goes, with sparks flying out everywhere! It's spinning around faster and faster! Red, orange, yellow, green, blue and purple sparks are flying out, making it look like a whirling rainbow. Then it slows down and comes to a stop. What a great display! What will come next?

Someone is handing out sparklers. Will you have a turn? Yes, you will. You walk with your parents over to a safe area. Your Dad holds out a match to light your sparkler. It starts to smoulder a little, but it doesn't light straight away. You wait patiently, and then a tiny spark comes away from your sparkler. It's going to start! Suddenly, the whole end of your sparkler erupts with tiny sparks! They are flying off everywhere! Quickly you turn and wave your sparkler in the air. The bright white sparks dazzle your eyes. You write your name in the air and watch as it magically stays there for you to read. You wave your arm in a big circle and watch the sparkling circles staying in the air. Then you begin to draw big squares, triangles and oblongs! It's so much fun. Oh no! The sparks are dying away. Little by little, the sparkler is going out. Now you're just standing there, holding a black sparkler stick! You give your sparkler stick to your Dad, who puts it in a big bucket of cold water.

The fireworks display has finished and it's time to go home. You can't wait until next year to see the wonderful fireworks again!

We're going to take three deep breaths again. Breathe in, hold, and slowly breathe out. Then again, breathe in, and out. Breathe in, and out.
Good. Now slowly sit up.
We've finished.
Well done.

Fireworks Night

Listening Comprehension

1. There are four kinds of fireworks. Draw a line to match each type of firework with its description.

1. Sparklers   a. Loud fizzing noise, silver and gold falling to the ground.

2. Catherine Wheel   b. Bang, whiz, pop! Red, blue and green stars falling.

3. Sparkling rain   c. Bright white sparks flying everywhere.

4. Sky rockets   d. Sparks flying around in a circle. Rainbow colours.

2. In which order did the fireworks come?

1st was   ....

2nd was   ....

3rd was   ....

4th was   ....

3. Draw a picture of each of the fireworks. Colour them in the correct colours.

Fireworks Night

Creative Expression

1. Fireworks can be fun, but they are very noisy! Write a list of words that describe the noises that fireworks make.

   ....

   ....

   ....

   ....

   ....

2. Write some sentences about a time you saw some fireworks.

   ....

   ....

   ....

   ....

   ....

   ....

3. Draw a picture of your favourite fireworks. Write some words on your picture to describe how it looks and sounds!

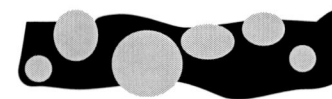

I'm A Bird

Hello children. It's time for our Learning To Listen story.
Lie down with your back on the mat or lean forward and put your head on your table.
Make sure you're not touching anyone. Close your eyes. Remember we are learning to actively listen for a sustained amount of time.
Now take a deep breath, hold it, and let it out slowly. Do it again, breathe in ... and out. Breathe in, and out. I want you to keep taking deep breaths while I read you a story.

Listen carefully.

Today you are going to be a bird. Imagine you're crouched down and your body is folded around. You're in an egg, and there's no room to move! Even though it's quiet and warm in your egg, it's time to get out. In the darkness, you peck the inside of your egg with your beak. It is hard, and you don't think you'll ever get out! But then your beak makes a tiny hole. You keep pecking, and suddenly a piece of shell breaks away. Light pours into the egg, and then the rest of it cracks away. You're out of your shell!

You look around you. There are two other eggs in the nest. They are pale blue, with little speckles on them. As you watch them, you see one start to wobble. Then you can hear a tap, tap, tapping noise, and the egg starts to shake. Out pops a little bird's beak, and then out pops the whole bird! It is your bird brother! You watch as the next egg begins to wobble. You listen to the tap, tap, tapping noise, and then you see the egg shake. Out pops another little bird. It is your bird sister!

You all start to peep excitedly as you see each other. Suddenly you are very hungry. What is there to eat in your nest? You look around, but there isn't anything but your shells. You and your brother and sister began to peep in your loudest voices. "Bring us some food!"

Suddenly, there is a rush of wings, and a big brown bird swoops down and lands on your nest. It is your mother! You are very pleased to see her because she has a big fat worm in her beak! You all peep noisily until she gives you each a piece of the worm. Yummy! Now you feel happy again!

You stay in your nest for many days. It is warm in here with your brother and sister bird. Your mother brings you food, and you start to grow bigger and bigger. Soon there is not much room in the nest for you and your brother and sister.

Then one day, your mother bird stops bringing your food. You start to get very hungry, and you peep very loudly, but still mother bird does not bring you food. It is time for you to leave the nest!

You climb to the edge of the nest. Your brother and sister bird follow you. You're very high up here! You can see a long way in every direction. You all stand on the edge of nest and stretch your wings. Who will go first?

Suddenly, your brother bird leaps from the nest. Down, down, down he falls, then suddenly he's doing it! He's flying! He circles around and lands on a branch.

Then your sister birds leaps from the nest too! Down, down she falls, and then suddenly she's flying too! Around she circles, and then she flies up and lands on a branch. It's your turn now. But you're scared! It looks such a long way down. What if you can't do it?

But then suddenly, you decide to do it. You leap off and down, down, down you fall. Oh no, you're going to hit the ground! But then you start to flap your wings, and you stop falling! You're flapping and then you're going up in the air! You're flying! You swoop around and around your tree, until finally landing by your brother and sister across from the nest!

You've done it! Now you can get food whenever you want. It's great being a bird!

We're going to take three deep breaths again. Breathe in, hold, and slowly breathe out. Then again, breathe in, and out. Breathe in, and out.
Good. Now slowly sit up.
We've finished.
Well done.

I'm A Bird

Listening Comprehension

1. Here are some sentences from the story. Circle True or False for each one.

a) It is hard to get out of your egg.   True False

b) There are four eggs in the nest with you.   True False

c) The eggs are yellow.   True False

d) You mother brings you a fly to eat.   True False

e) Your mother stops bringing food.   True False

f) Your sister flies away first.   True False

g) You crash onto the ground.   True False

h) You can fly!   True False

2. Answer these questions.

a) How did it feel to live in the shell?..

....

b) How did it feel to live in the nest? ....

....

c) How did you feel before you flew? ....

....

d) How did you feel after your flew? ....

....

3. Draw a picture as described in the story of:

the eggs in the nest	the baby birds in the nest	flying from the nest

I'm A Bird

Creative Expression

1. In the story, the bird was fed a worm by his mother.
   What other kinds of food do you think a bird would eat? Write a list.

   ....

   ....

   ....

   ....

2. Imagine you're a bird about to fly for the first time.
   How would you feel:

   before flying? ....

   ....

   while you are flying? ....

   ....

   after flying? ....

   ....

3. Imagine you are a baby seabird. It would be different to living in a tree. Write a story about a baby bird that lives in a nest at the top of a cliff.

   ....

   ....

   ....

   ....

   ....

   ....

   ....

   ....

   ....

   ....

   ....

   ....

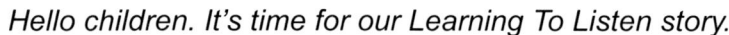

I'm A Giant

Hello children. It's time for our Learning To Listen story.
Lie down with your back on the mat or lean forward and put your head on your table.
Make sure you're not touching anyone. Close your eyes. Remember we are learning to
actively listen for a sustained amount of time.
Now take a deep breath, hold it, and let it out slowly. Do it again, breathe in ... and out. Breathe in, and
out. I want you to keep taking deep breaths while I read you a story.

Listen carefully.

It's a lovely day, and you're lying out in your backyard. It's so warm out there that you start to feel sleepy. Your eyes close, and soon you're asleep. Then you have a very strange dream! Your arms and legs are tingling all over. It feels like they are growing! Your eyes fly open, and you look at your body. And you see that you are growing! Your body is growing bigger and bigger! You have turned into a giant!
You sit up and look around you. Even sitting down, you are the size of your house!
Very carefully, you stand up. Where should you go? You take a step forward and see the road. You walk down the road, being very careful not to stand on any cars. But tiny people are jumping out of their cars and pointing up at you! It is very tricky. You need to get to an open space before you stand on someone!
Then you see the beach. You take a long giant's step and you're in the water! But it's only up to your knees. There are three little sailing boats around you on the water, and when they see you they start to yell. You wonder why they are yelling, but then you see. When you got into the water, you made some waves. They will turn the sailing boats over! Quickly you reach down and pick up the three little sailing boats in your hand. When the waves have gone, you carefully place them back into the water. The sailers are happy now! They wave to you as you step out of the sea. It is not safe in the water. But where can you go?
You will go to the countryside. There will be space there. You walk down the beach and then turn into the countryside. It is very peaceful here, with rolling green fields. There are not so many people to worry about now! But there are animals. And they do not seem happy to see a giant either!
Tiny cows moo at you, tiny pigs oink at you, tiny horses neigh at you, and tiny sheep baa at you. They run around your feet, and you have to step very carefully so you don't knock any over. It is not safe in the countryside. But where can you go?
You will go to the mountains. There will be space there. You take ten big steps, and then you're standing by the mountains. Ten more big steps, and you're halfway up the mountain. Then you take ten more big steps, and you're on top of the mountain. What a great view! You can see everywhere you've just been – the town, the ocean and the countryside. It is very peaceful here on top of the mountain. You do not have to watch out for people, or sailers, or animals. The only trouble is that it is getting cold. The longer you sit there, the colder you are getting. Suddenly you feel something on your nose. It is icicles! They are forming on your nose! This is not a good place for a giant to be.
It's time to head down the mountain again. When you reach the bottom, you suddenly feel very tired. You lie down and close your eyes. Then you have a very strange dream. It feels like your body is shrinking! Your eyes fly open, and you look down. You're back to your normal size again, and you're back in your backyard. Thank goodness. Being a giant was tricky!

We're going to take three deep breaths again. Breathe in, hold, and slowly breathe out. Then again,
breathe in, and out. Breathe in, and out.
Good. Now slowly sit up.
We've finished.
Well done.

I'm A Giant

Listening Comprehension

1. Read the sentences. Put a circle around either True or False.

a) You are lying in your backyard.   True False

b) You shrink until you are tiny.   True False

c) You stand on a car.   True False

d) There are five sailing boats.   True False

e) The cows are happy to see you.   True False

f) There are icicles on your nose.   True False

1. Choose a word from the following list to complete the sentences.

steps	dream	colder	cows	waves

a) You have a very strange ....

b) When you got into the water, you made ....

c) Tiny .... moo at you.

d) You take ten .... and you're on top of the mountain.

e) The longer you sit there, the .... you are getting.

3. Draw a map of your journey as a giant. Mark on it – your house, the road, the sea, the countryside and the mountain.

I'm A Giant

Creative Expression

1. It would be tricky to be a giant but there would be the good things about being a giant too. Write a list of them.

   ....

   ....

   ....

   ....

   ....

   ....

   ....

2. **What would happen if your best friend was a giant?**

   Write a story about the things you would do and the places you would go with your giant friend.

   ....

   ....

   ....

   ....

   ....

   ....

   ....

3. **Draw a picture of you and your giant friend.**

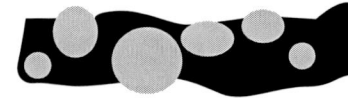 

Hello children. It's time for our Learning To Listen story.
Lie down with your back on the mat or lean forward and put your head on your table.
Make sure you're not touching anyone. Close your eyes. Remember we are learning to actively listen for a sustained amount of time.
Now take a deep breath, hold it, and let it out slowly. Do it again, breathe in ... and out. Breathe in, and out. I want you to keep taking deep breaths while I read you a story.

Listen carefully.

Today we're going to take a rainbow ride. Just imagine you're walking over some beautiful green hills. It's easy to walk, it's just been raining but the sun is just coming out from behind the clouds. You can smell the lovely fresh scents of the countryside.

You look up, and then you see it. A huge rainbow, stretching right across the sky in front of you. The colours are so clear and bright, and you look at them in wonder. Red, orange, yellow, green, blue, indigo and violet. You want to get closer, so you keep walking towards the rainbow. It looks so close to you now, as if you could just reach out and touch it. You put your hand out, and then suddenly, you're there! You're inside the rainbow!

Violet rays of light are all around you. Everywhere you look is a soft pretty purple. It smells sweet, like lavender and lilac flowers. It's so beautiful you could stay here forever. But then you push off with your feet, and suddenly you're soaring upwards. You land on the next colour of the rainbow!

Indigo rays of light are all around you. Everywhere you look is a deep, dark purple. It reminds you of royalty, and of grapes and aubergines. It's so beautiful you could stay here forever. But then you push off with your feet, and suddenly you're soaring upwards. You land on the next colour of the rainbow!

Blue rays of light are all around you. The blue is everywhere, like the deepest ocean and the clearest sky. It is cool. It's so beautiful you could stay here forever. But then you push off with your feet, and suddenly you're soaring upwards. You land on the next colour of the rainbow!

Green rays of light are all around you. It's like being in a dense forest of tall green trees. Greens of all colours; emerald, sage and jade. It's so beautiful you could stay here forever. But then you push off with your feet, and suddenly you're soaring upwards. You land on the next part of the rainbow!

Yellow rays of light are all around you. It's like standing in the light of the warmest sun. It's the colour of daffodils, butter and canaries. It's so beautiful you could stay here forever. But then you push off with your feet, and suddenly you're soaring upwards. You land on the next part of the rainbow!

Orange rays of light are all around you. It's like a beautiful sunrise. It's like carrots and pumpkins, peaches and apricots. It's so beautiful you could stay here forever. But then you push off with your feet, and suddenly you're soaring upwards. You land on the next part of the rainbow!

Red rays of light are all around you. It's like the glow of a fire, and the end of a sunset. It's the colour of rubies and tomatoes and roses. It's hot here, like fire. It's so beautiful you could stay here forever. But then you push off with your feet, and suddenly you're soaring upwards. You land on the top of the rainbow!

It's slippery, and you start sliding down on the arc of the rainbow, and you're coming down fast! Faster and faster you slide, until suddenly, you reach the end of the rainbow and you tumble onto the ground.

You turn around to see the rainbow, but it has gone. You're standing back on the green hills, smelling the fresh country air.

What a wonderful rainbow ride!

We're going to take three deep breaths again. Breathe in, hold, and slowly breathe out. Then again, breathe in, and out. Breathe in, and out.
Good. Now slowly sit up.
We've finished.
Well done.

Rainbow Ride

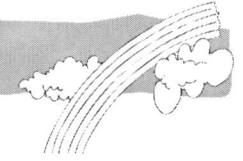

Listening Comprehension

1. Name the seven colours of the rainbow.

_____

_____

_____

_____

_____

_____

_____

2. For each colour give two examples of items that were named in the story 'Rainbow Ride'.

– _____   _____

– _____   _____

– _____   _____

– _____   _____

– _____   _____

– _____   _____

– _____   _____

3. True or False

a) It is a hot, dry day.   True False

b) You walk inside the rainbow.   True False

c) The rainbow is slippery.   True False

d) As you walk home you look at the rainbow.   True False

4. Draw a picture of the rainbow in the story. Name the bands of colour. Draw you sliding down the top of the rainbow.

Rainbow Ride

Creative Expression

1. Choose your favourite colour of the rainbow.

Write a paragraph about what it would be like to live in your favourite colour. What would it feel like? What would it smell like? What would you see?

....

....

....

....

....

....

2. Find alternate names for the colours of the rainbow. The first one for each colour has been done for you. (You might like to use a thesaurus.)

Red – rose,

Orange – apricot,

Yellow – mustard,

Green – olive,

Blue – sapphire,

Indigo – aubergine,

Violet – mauve,

3. Make up your own personal rainbow.

You can't use any of the following names – red, orange, yellow, green, blue, indigo or violet. Draw it in the box below.

Hello children. It's time for our Learning To Listen story.
Lie down with your back on the mat or lean forward and put your head on your table.
Make sure you're not touching anyone. Close your eyes. Remember we are learning to actively listen for a sustained amount of time.
Now take a deep breath, hold it, and let it out slowly. Do it again, breathe in ... and out. Breathe in, and out. I want you to keep taking deep breaths while I read you a story.

Listen carefully.

Today you are going on a train trip. You are feeling excited because you love trains, and the best thing of all is that you are going on a steam train! You love the sights, sounds and smells of a steam train. You arrive at the station early so you don't miss that train! But when you get there, you can't see the steam train anywhere! You check your watch again, but the time is the same, and you know you aren't late. You stand on the platform and wait. There are many other people waiting too, so hopefully the steam train will be here soon.

Suddenly, you hear something! A toot, toot, tooting sound! It's the train whistle! Then you hear another sound. Clackety clack! Clackety clack! It's the sound of the train riding on the rails! Then you hear another sound. It's a slow hisssssssssssing sound, the sound of steam coming out of a train!

And then you see it! It comes around the corner and into the station! It's a huge black locomotive, with white steam belching from the stack! The sounds are very loud now, especially the toot, toot of the whistle from the driver!

Everyone is waiting to get on the train, but first all the people on the train have to get off! You wait until everyone is off, and the stationmaster says, "All aboard! All aboard!".

You choose the carriage at the very back and climb up the narrow stairs onto the train. Then you choose a window seat, and slide along the shiny red leather. Now you can see the whole train right there in front of you.

Next the ticket master comes down. "Tickets please!" he calls in his big voice. You give him your red ticket, and he clicks it with his clipper. "Enjoy your ride," he says with a smile.

You wait for a few more minutes until all the passengers have taken their seats. And then you hear the toot, toot, toot of the whistle. It's time to go! You look out the window and see the steam puffing up as the engineer starts to pull the train out of the station. There's a jolt, and a squeal of the tracks, and you're moving! You're moving out of the station, and you wave to the people standing on the platform. Goodbye, goodbye!

You're off! You're moving through the countryside on a beautiful summer's day! The cows that are chewing the grass in their paddocks look up and stare at you as you clatter passed them on the tracks. You hear the toot toot of the whistle again, this time to warn some cars that we are going to cross the road. You see the crossing as the train zooms past. You're going very fast now! You can hear the train on the rails going clickety clack! Clickety clack! The steam is puffing out in great white clouds from the top of the train. Then you're going around a big sweeping corner, and into a tunnel! It's dark inside the tunnel! You can't even see your hand in front of your face! You can smell the strong scent of the coal and smoke from the steam train too. Then you're out in the bright sunshine again. And you're slowing now, slowing down, as you come back to the station again. The driver blows the horn again, toot, toot! There is a loud hisssssssssssing sound as the train comes to a stop at the platform. Wow! That was fun! You think you'll stay on and have another turn. What a great ride on a steam train!

We're going to take three deep breaths again. Breathe in, hold, and slowly breathe out. Then again, breathe in, and out. Breathe in, and out.
Good. Now slowly sit up.
We've finished.
Well done.

Listening Comprehension

1. Draw a line to match the question in A to the answer in B.

A	B
a) You arrive early so that	go past the cars.
b) You hear the train	the back carriage.
c) The train comes	into the station
d) You climb into	you don't miss the train.
e) The ticket master	before you see it.
f) The train toots as you	coal and smoke.
g) In the tunnel you can smell	clips your ticket.

2. The train is very noisy! Choose a word or words from the list to describe all the sounds that you heard.

clackety clack	toot toot	hisssssssssssss	All aboard!	Tickets please!

a) The station master says, ".."

b) The ticket master says, ".."

c) The train goes ....

d) The horn goes ....

e) The steam goes ....

3. Number the boxes to put these statements in the correct order.

a) The people get off the train. ☐

b) You stand on the platform. ☐

c) You get on the train. ☐

d) The train comes. ☐

4. Draw a picture of your favourite part of the story.

Riding The Steam Train

Creative Expression

1. On the train you went for a ride through the countryside. Where else could you go in a steam train? Make a list of all the places you can think of. Draw a picture beside each one.

....

....

....

....

....

....

2. Choose the place you'd like to go the most. Write a story about travelling there on the train.

....

....

....

....

....

....

....

....

....

3. Would you like to be the engineer, the station master, or the ticket master? Write a paragraph about your favourite job.

....

....

....

....

Seaside Walk

Hello children. It's time for our Learning To Listen story.
Lie down with your back on the mat or lean forward and put your head on your table.
Make sure you're not touching anyone. Close your eyes. Remember we are learning to actively listen for a sustained amount of time.
Now take a deep breath, hold it, and let it out slowly. Do it again, breathe in ... and out. Breathe in, and out. I want you to keep taking deep breaths while I read you a story.

Listen carefully.

Today we are going for a walk at the beach. It's a lovely winter's day. The sky is a deep dark blue and the sea is sparkling. There is a cool breeze, and you're glad you're wearing your warm clothes and hat.

As you walk along the beach, you can hear many sounds. The first sound you hear is the birds. There are seagulls swooping overhead, calling to each other. There are more seagulls sitting up on the sand dunes. They squawk at you as you walk closer to them. Suddenly, they start flapping their wings, and then they launch themselves into the air. Up, up, up they go, to join the rest of the seagulls flying over the sea.

The other sound you can hear is the ocean. The waves are small today, and you can hear them slap down onto the sand. Then there is a sucking sound as the water rolls back to the sea again. As you walk along, you hear the slap, suck, slap, suck of the waves.

There is a lot to see on the beach today. The tide is out now, but when the tide was high, it brought piles of debris onto the sand. You start to look through it. There are long green leaves of seaweed, which smells like the sea. You poke it with your finger, and it is cold and slimy!

Then you see some driftwood. You pick up a piece and rub your hand on it. It is so smooth! This wood has been in the ocean so long, it has been worn smooth by the water. You put the driftwood down.

There are many different kinds of shells, small curved white shells and long curly orange shells. You wonder what kind of creatures used to live in them. Are they still in there? You stare inside, but you can't see anything, so you put them down again.

You keep walking along, and you notice that there are more rocks and pebbles along this part of the beach. Some are huge rocks which are deeply buried in the sand, and others are small pebbles sitting on the top. You pick up a flat pebble. It is quite heavy in your hand. You walk closer to the water, and then with a flick of your wrist, you send the pebble flying over the water. It skips over the surface twice before it disappears under the water.

Then you notice that you're walking towards some flat rocks. As you get closer, you see that there are rock pools there too. You walk over to them. At first there isn't much to see, except for some seaweed growing around the edges of the pool. But as you stand there, you see something. There are some tiny little fish in the rock pool! They are swimming together up and down the side of the pool. They look silvery in the winter sun.

Then you see something else. Two big pinchers poke out from behind a rock. Then comes a flat shell, and four legs. It's a crab! You stand very still and you watch him as he comes out from under the rock. The crab sits in the middle of the rock pool, his pinchers out. Suddenly, a seagull swoops over your head, and squawks at you. You watch the seagull, and when you turn your head back to the rock pool, you notice that the crab has gone! What a clever crab!

It's time to go home now. You turn and go back along the beach. What a great place for a winter's walk!

We're going to take three dee

s again. Breathe in, hold, and slowly breathe out. Then again, breathe in, and out. Breathe in, and out. Good. Now slowly sit up.
We've finished.
Well done.

Seaside Walk

Listening Comprehension

1. What did you see on your seaside walk? Draw a circle around them, and colour them in.

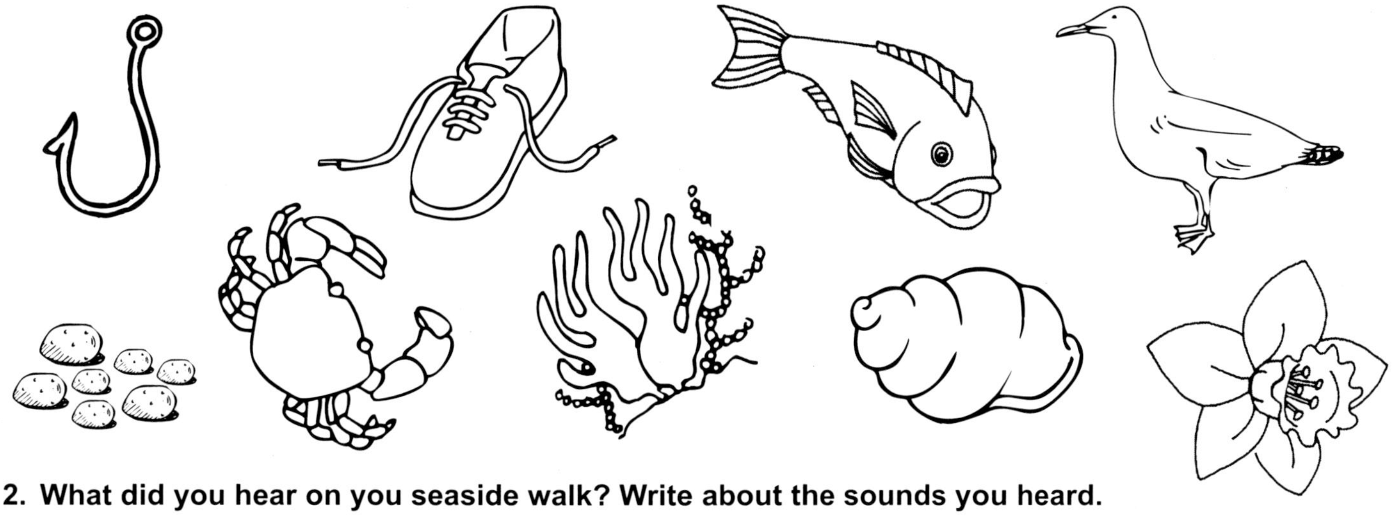

2. What did you hear on you seaside walk? Write about the sounds you heard.

Seagulls ....

....

Waves ....

....

3. What did you see in the rock pool? Write the three things that you saw. Then draw a picture of the rock pool, and the things in it.

In the rock pool, I saw –

....

....

....

Creative Expression

1. Look at these footprints. Who has been walking along the beach?

2. What other creatures might be hiding in the rock pools? Draw a picture of your own rock pool.

3. Write a story about a time you went to the seaside. What did you do? What did you see? What did you hear? What did you smell?

....

....

....

....

....

....

....

....

....

The Dolls' House

Hello children. It's time for our Learning To Listen story.
Lie down with your back on the mat or lean forward and put your head on your table.
Make sure you're not touching anyone. Close your eyes. Remember we are learning to actively listen for a sustained amount of time.
Now take a deep breath, hold it, and let it out slowly. Do it again, breathe in ... and out. Breathe in, and out. I want you to keep taking deep breaths while I read you a story.

Listen carefully.

You've just moved into a new house. It's been fun exploring the garden and the neighbourhood. But when you wake up on the first weekend, it is pouring with rain. What should you do? Then your Mother says to you, "Why don't you go up to the attic. There are some things up there that the old owners left behind."

What a good idea. You walk into the hallway, and you see a narrow door in the wall. You open it. It's very dark in there, so you switch on the light. Now you can see a narrow staircase, with steps leading upwards. You start climbing the stairs and they creak noisily under your feet.

Before long you're at the top. There is a dusty old window at the far end of the attic, which lets in a little light. You can see odd shapes around the sides of the room. When you walk closer you see that everything is covered in sheets. You lift a sheet off, and see an old bicycle, some old garden tools, and a painting of a lady in a frame. You put the sheet back. Then you see a big square shape. What could be under this sheet?

Carefully you lift it off. And there before you is the most wonderful doll house. The walls are made out of wood, and the roof is made from tiles. It's painted just like a real house, and it even has a leafy vine painted up the side of the house. Very gently you open up the doors on the front. Inside there are two levels, joined by a tiny staircase. In each room there are tiny pieces of furniture, including a little white bath in the bathroom, beds in the bedrooms, and a tiny table in the dining room, complete with a dinner set. There is a baby's room with a tiny cot. There are tiny lights hanging from the ceilings, and patterned wallpaper on the walls. It's all so wonderful to see.

Then you notice a little hinge on the roof of the doll house. What could that be? Carefully, you lift open part of the roof. You can't see very well, so you put your hand it and take out what is in there. It's three tiny dolls! There is a father doll, a mother doll, and a baby doll. They are beautifully painted, with faces that look like they are real!

Carefully, you place the dolls into the doll house. You put the baby in the cot, and the Mother doll and the Father doll in the dining room. Then you sit back to see how it looks.

What a shock you get when the Mother and Father doll begin to speak! "That's better," says the Mother doll. "I do like to be back in the house again."

"Yes," says the Father doll. "Very nice indeed."

You sit there feeling so surprised. The dolls have come alive! You don't want to move unless you frighten them. Then you hear the sound of the tiny baby doll crying. You watch as the Mother doll stands up and walks to the baby's room. She picks the baby up, and rocks him. "There, there, little baby," says the Mother doll. Then to your surprise, she turns around and smiles at you!

Just then you hear footsteps on the attic stairs. It's your Mother! You quickly look back at the dolls, but they are not moving now. Their faces are still. They are proper dolls again. As you watch them though, the Father doll winks at you. You hope that one day, you will be able to visit the doll family again.

We're going to take three deep breaths again. Breathe in, hold, and slowly breathe out. Then again, breathe in, and out. Breathe in, and out.
Good. Now slowly sit up.
We've finished.
Well done.

The Dolls' House

Listening Comprehension

1. **What do you find under the sheets in the attic? Draw a circle around the correct pictures. Colour them in.**

2. **What does the dolls' house look like? Choose a word to finish the sentence.**

wallpaper	staircase	tiles	wood	leafy vine	white bath

   a) The walls are made of ....

   b) The roof is made from ....

   c) Up the side of the house is a ....

   d) The two levels are joined by a ....

   e) In the bathroom is a little ....

   f) On the walls is patterned ....

3. **Draw a picture of the doll house from the story.**

The Dolls' House

Creative Expression

1. Imagine that you are a doll living in a doll house.

What would be good about being a doll?

....

....

....

What would not be good about being a doll?

....

....

....

Would you like to be a doll?

....

....

....

2. If a doll could talk, what would you want to know? Write five questions you would ask.

— ....

— ....

— ....

— ....

— ....

3. Draw a picture of one of the dolls from the story.

Hello children. It's time for our Learning To Listen story.
Lie down with your back on the mat or lean forward and put your head on your table.
Make sure you're not touching anyone. Close your eyes. Remember we are learning to actively listen for a sustained amount of time.
Now take a deep breath, hold it, and let it out slowly. Do it again, breathe in ... and out. Breathe in, and out. I want you to keep taking deep breaths while I read you a story.

Listen carefully.

You are in your bedroom. You're sitting on your bed reading a book. But suddenly you see something from the corner of your eye. You look out of the window. Yes, there is something there. A ball of light, and it's sparkling and shimmering at the end of the garden!

You walk out of your house and down the back track into the garden. The light is still there, hovering mysteriously under the tall trees. Your feet crunch through some old yellow leaves on the track. And suddenly, the light disappears!

You stop walking now, and stand very still. Very slowly, the light starts to appear again. Soon it's as bright as before, and it's sparkling and shimmering more than ever! You want to see what is at the end of your garden, so very quietly you tiptoe down the track, being careful not to stand on any more crunchy leaves.

Soon, you're nearly on the edge of the light. You could reach out and touch that beautiful sparkly light, but you decide not to. You move forward, and stand behind a big forest. You peep around to see what is making that wonderful light. What a sight you see!

There are hundreds of tiny fairies in your garden. Each one is only as high as your tallest finger. They are dressed in the most beautiful clothes. The girl fairies wear long glittering dresses in all the colours of the rainbow. The boys are wearing beautiful tailored pants, and tiny vests. They all have long silvery wings, and when they move, bursts of shimmering stars appear. This is what is making the light!

The fairies are sitting on a group of toadstools that is shaped like a ring. The fairies are so tiny, that there are ten of them sitting on each toadstool. They are all chattering in high-pitched voices, and they don't seem to have noticed you standing behind the forest at all.

Suddenly, they all stop chattering. Have they seen you? But then you relax as you notice they are looking at an empty toadstool. And then suddenly they all burst out into a loud cheer. You watch as a beautiful fairy flies down and lands on the toadstool. Her gown is gleaming white, and she wears a tiny gold crown on her head. A little while later another fairy flies down. He is wearing a suit of gleaming gold, and he also wears a tiny crown on his head. All of the other fairies bow low. This must be the King and Queen of the Fairies!

You lean forward to listen as they speak. The Queen speaks first. She thanks them all for coming today on this special occasion. She says that they are not only beautiful, but they have proven themselves to be the kindest and wisest of all the fairies.

Then the King flies up into the air. He waves his hand in the air as he speaks. You are all to be honoured, he says, by being given a special golden star. You must wear this always, so it will be known you are the best fairies in the land.

Then with a flick of his wrist, suddenly all of the fairies are wearing a beautiful golden star! The fairies all cheer with delight. You are so happy for them, that you forget you are supposed to be hiding, and you start to clap your hands. But the moment you do, the fairies all turn and look at you. You've been found! And in that second, the fairies magically disappear! All you're looking at is a ring of toadstools at the bottom of your garden.

We're going to take three deep breaths again. Breathe in, hold, and slowly breathe out. Then again, breathe in, and out. Breathe in, and out.
Good. Now slowly sit up.
We've finished.
Well done.

The Fairy Ring

Listening Comprehension

1. Here are some statements about the story. Are they true or false? Put a circle around the correct answer.

a) You are playing a card game on your bed.   True False

b) You see a light in your garden.   True False

c) You reach out and touch the light.   True False

d) The fairies are dressed in old rags.   True False

e) The King and Queen are wearing crowns.   True False

f) The fairies are given a special golden sun.   True False

g) The fairies disappear when you clap.   True False

2. Finish the sentences from the story by choosing an answer from below.

tallest finger	rainbow	toadstools	vests
white	forest	gold	yellow leaves

a) Your feet crunch on the ....

b) You hide behind a big ....

c) The fairies are sitting on ....

d) The fairies dresses are the colour of the ....

e) The boy fairies are wearing ....

f) The King is wearing a suit of ....

g) The Queen is wearing a dress of ....

h) The fairies are as high as your ....

3. Draw a picture of:

a fairy	the King	the Queen

Creative Expression

1. The fairies in the story all received a golden star for being the best fairies in the land. The King said that they were not only beautiful, but also kind and wise. Write a story about a fairy that has done something kind for someone.

   My fairy's name is ....

   A time my fairy helped someone was..

   ....

   ....

   ....

   ....

   ....

   ....

   ....

   ....

   ....

   ....

2. **Draw a picture of your fairy.**

The Gingerbread Cottage

Listen carefully.

Today you are going on a walk through a forest. The track winds through the trees, and as you walk you can hear birds singing. Suddenly you come to a fork in the track. The track to the left is wide, and you can see patches of sun on the ground. The track to the right is narrow and dark, and you can't see very far down it. Which track should you take? You choose the track to the right. You are very interested to see what might be at the end of such a narrow winding track.

As you walk along, you notice that it's much quieter now. The birds that were singing before have gone. And it's getting darker and darker. The track is getting narrower and narrower. Just when you think you won't be able to go any further, you see light up ahead. You keep walking and suddenly you're in a clearing. And in that clearing is the most wonderful sight! It's a gingerbread cottage! The walls are made of golden gingerbread, and colourful strips of blue and pink icing surround it. The windows are made of licorice, and the doorknob is a chocolate button. You walk right up to it. The smell is amazing; you just have to have a taste of that wonderful gingerbread. So you take a small nibble of the letterbox. Mmmmm! It's delicious! Suddenly you hear somebody coming through the forest! What should you do?

You see that the door to the gingerbread cottage is slightly open. You run up the track, through the door, and into the cottage. You've arrived in the middle of a big kitchen. Luckily for you, there are long curtains at the window, so you quickly stand behind one. You're just in time, because in comes the owner of the gingerbread cottage. It's a witch! A tall skinny witch with a black cloak and a long pointed hat! She is carrying a broom, and in the other hand she has a bunch of wild flowers.

"I've got them," she says. At first you think she is talking to you, but then you see a big black cat sitting on a mat in front of a fire. The cat has huge green eyes, and you know that the cat must have seen you hide behind the curtains! It's lucky that cats can't talk!

The witch crosses the room and stands in front of a pot that is boiling over the fire. She breaks four blue flowers from their stems, and drops them into the water. Next she drops in a whistle and a four-leaf clover. Then to your surprise, she takes a small pair of scissors, and cuts off the ends of the cat's whiskers. She drops them into the pot and begins to stir it around and around. She's whispering a spell as she stirs and blue smoke starts to rise from the pot.

"It's ready," she says to the cat. "Your sore throat will be fixed. One spoon of this, and you'll be talking to me again."

Oh no! The cat is going to speak? You'll be found! It's time to move! Luckily the witch has her back to you, and even more lucky, the door is still open. You tiptoe across the kitchen floor, and you don't stop even when you hear a loud miaow! Once you're out of the cottage, you start to run as fast as you can! Down the winding track, back to the fork in the track, and out of the forest.

Phew! That was close. Next time you think you'll take the easier track!

The Gingerbread Cottage

Listening Comprehension

1. Draw a line to match the question on the left with the answer on the right.

a) Which track do you take?   A gingerbread cottage

b) What do you find in the clearing?   Behind the curtains

c) What is the doorknob made of?   The right track

d) Where do you hide?   A sore throat

e) Who comes in the door?   The cat's whiskers

f) What is the last thing the witch   A witch
   puts in the pot?

g) What is wrong with the cat?   A chocolate button

2. Put a circle around the items that the witch put in the pot for her spell. Colour them in.

3. Match the correct colour.

pink	blue	golden
black	brown	green

a) The gingerbread is ....

b) The icing is .... and ....

c) The chocolate buttons are ....

d) The witch's cloak is.............................

e) The eyes of the cat are huge and.............

f) The flowers and smoke are....................

4. Draw the gingerbread cottage.

The Gingerbread Cottage

Creative Expression

1. Answer these questions.

What do you think the cat would say if it could talk?

....

....

What do you think the witch would say if she saw you?

....

....

What might have happened next?

....

....

2. Make up your own spell.

What would your spell do?

....

What would you put into your spell?

....

....

Write some magic words to say over your spell.

....

....

Imagine your own gingerbread cottage. What would it be made out from?

....

....

Draw a picture of it.

The Kite

Hello children. It's time for our Learning To Listen story.
Lie down with your back on the mat or lean forward and put your head on your table.
Make sure you're not touching anyone. Close your eyes. Remember we are learning to actively listen for a sustained amount of time.
Now take a deep breath, hold it, and let it out slowly. Do it again, breathe in ... and out. Breathe in, and out. I want you to keep taking deep breaths while I read you a story.

Listen carefully.

Today you're going to the park to fly your kite. You've been waiting for the perfect day, and this is it! It's sunny and the sky is blue, and there is a warm breeze blowing. Which kite will you take? The small blue one? The medium-sized green one? Or will it be the big red one? Yes. You pick the big red one. You like it because it has long red streamers attached to the end for a tail.

You pick up the kite, and carry it down to the park. The wind blows the kite, and you pull it close to your body and hold onto it tightly. When you arrive at the park, you look around to check if there are any overhead power lines. Luckily there aren't. Great! It's time to fly your kite.

First, you check which way the wind is blowing. Then you turn your back into the wind, and let out a little string. Your kite leaps around as the wind lifts it. You can hear the rustle of the tail, and the flap, flap, flap of your kite as the wind rattles it. Slowly you let out more string. Your kite is rising into the sky. It's ready to go! You let out a lot of string now, and your kite climbs higher and higher! The long red tail is waving from side to side as the kite soars through the sky.

Now the wind seems to be getting stronger. And your kite wants to ride it! It's tugging on the string, like a fish on a line! The wind is pushing at you too, but you're holding on tightly to the handle of your kite. You won't let go! And suddenly, your feet are lifting off the ground! The kite is pulling you up into the sky!

Higher and higher you go. You look up, and see your big red kite with its flapping red tail high in the sky above you. When you look down, you can see the park beneath you. It's a long way down! But you're not scared. You're holding on tightly to your kite, and you won't let go.

It's very noisy up here with your kite. The wind is whistling in your ears, the tails on your kite are rustling, and your kite is going flap, flap, flap.

Then the wind starts blowing you along. You're not going up anymore, but you're going forwards. You leave the park behind, and then you're flying over the roads far below you. When you look down, you see you're flying over your house! It looks so small from up here!

Then you've passed your house, and you're flying over your school. You see your classroom, and the staffroom, and library. Then you're passing the school, and heading towards the shops. You can even see tiny people, rushing around down there!

You call out to them, but you are so high up in the air that no one can hear you.

Then you've passed your school, and you're coming around. It seems like the wind has changed direction and it's blowing you back. Yes, you're over the park again! And the wind is losing its strength. Your kite is starting to come down, and so are you. Down, down, down you come. You look and see the ground rushing up towards you. Then your feet are on the grass again, and you tumble over. Your kite lands safely on the ground beside you. Quickly you roll the string up again. Wow! That was an amazing kite ride!

We're going to take three deep breaths again. Breathe in, hold, and slowly breathe out. Then again, breathe in, and out. Breathe in, and out.
Good. Now slowly sit up.
We've finished.
Well done.

The Kite

Listening Comprehension

1. Look at the following sentences from the story. They are mixed up.

a) The kite flies over the school.

b) You carry your kite to the park.

c) You pick the big red kite.

d) The kite flies over the shops.

e) The kite comes down again.

f) The kite pulls you off the ground.

Write them again in the correct order.

1st ....

2nd ....

3rd ....

4th ....

5th ....

6th ....

2. Draw a picture of the kite you chose to fly. Colour it in. Don't forget the long tail!

3. Put a circle around the correct answer.

a) Did you choose the blue kite?   Yes   No

b) What did you look for at the park?   Power lines   Trees

c) Did the people hear you call out?   Yes   No

d) What did you fly over?   School   Sea

The Kite

Creative Expression

1. Imagine you had your own wonderful kite. What does it look like? What colour is it? What does it tail look like? Write about it.

....

....

....

....

....

....

....

....

2. What if your kite took you for a ride? Choose three places you would like to fly over.

....

....

....

3. Draw a map of your kite's track. Mark on it the places you would like to fly over on the way. Draw a picture of your kite with you hanging on underneath it.

The Magic Carousel

Hello children. It's time for our Learning To Listen story.
Lie down with your back on the mat or lean forward and put your head on your table.
Make sure you're not touching anyone. Close your eyes. Remember we are learning to actively listen for a sustained amount of time.
Now take a deep breath, hold it, and let it out slowly. Do it again, breathe in ... and out. Breathe in, and out. I want you to keep taking deep breaths while I read you a story.

Listen carefully.

Today we are going to the fair. You are feeling so excited, because the fair is your favourite place in the world to visit.

Now you're here, you're standing at the gates, and what a wonderful sight. It's just starting to get dark, and the fairground is lit up in colourful lights. There is a roller coaster, a Ferris wheel, a giant slide, and a cup and saucer ride. You can hear the happy screams from people riding on them.

But you want to find the best ride of all. You walk through the crowds of people, and smell the candyfloss and the hot dogs. They smell delicious, but you keep walking. And then you see it. The carousel! It is a huge merry-go-round, and it's lit up all over with gold and red flashing lights. On the carousel are the most beautiful horses. The horses are all the colours of the rainbow!

You walk up the steps, and onto the carousel. Which horse should you pick? They are all so beautiful. But then you see one. It is purple, gold and red, and it looks like a horse that a king or queen might ride. You walk over to it, and gently rub the horse's nose. You are sure that the horse's eyes are looking at you.

You climb up onto the carousel horse. Wow! You hold onto the pole, and you feel as tall as a castle! Then the music starts up. It is wonderful music that makes you want to dance. And then the carousel starts to move! Slowly at first, round and round, and your horse is going up and down. Then it starts going faster, and faster!

You wave to everyone as you go around and around. It feels great to have the wind in your hair. You are going so fast now, and you hold on to the horse's mane. Then suddenly you feel something strange. The horse's mane is real hair! And the horse's head starts to move up and down. Your horse is real! Then with a jolt, your horse jumps off the carousel, and into the air. And you are flying up, up, up into the sky.

You can see the fair beneath you, spread out with all the coloured lights. You are not afraid, because you know you are safe riding your wonderful horse. The horse rides higher into the night sky, and you feel like you can almost touch the sparkling stars. The wind is whistling through your hair, blowing it everywhere. It's starting to get cold now, up here in the sky, and you start to shiver.

Your horse feels it, and he begins to come down. Down, down, down. Back towards the earth again, back to the glittering lights of the fairground. You can see the roller coaster, the Ferris wheel, the giant slide and the cup and saucer ride. Then you see the carousel, with the beautiful gold and red lights. Down you go, and then with a clatter of hooves, you're back on the carousel. You're still going round and round, but it's slower now. The horse's mane is not real anymore, and you're holding onto the pole again.

Slower, and slower, then the carousel stops. It is time to go now. You climb off your horse, and gently rub its nose. "Thank you for the wonderful ride," you whisper. The horse doesn't say anything, but you're sure you see a twinkle in its eye.

You climb down the steps, and walk away from the carousel. That was such great fun! What a magical carousel ride!

We're going to take three deep breaths again. Breathe in, hold, and slowly breathe out. Then again, breathe in, and out. Breathe in, and out.
Good. Now slowly sit up.
We've finished.
Well done.

Listening Comprehension

1. Put a circle around the things you saw at the fair. Colour them in.

2. Draw a line to match the questions in List A with the answers in List B.

A	B
You can smell	and you shiver.
Two other rides are	and thank him for the ride.
The carousel is	off the carousel.
Your horse is	gold and red.
Your horse jumps	hot-dogs and candyfloss.
You feel as if you could	the roller coaster and the slide.
It is getting cold	purple, gold and red.
You climb off your horse	touch the stars.

3. Answer the questions with a Yes or No.

A) Is it night? ....

B) Can you smell hot chips? ....

C) Is your favourite ride the big slide? ....

D) Do you choose the green horse? ....

E) Does your horse jump into the air? ....

F) Are you scared? ....

G) Is it hot in the sky? ....

H) Is there a twinkle in the horse's eye? ....

The Magic Carousel

Creative Expression

1. Imagine you are going to the fair or an amusement park.

What is your favourite ride?..

Why? ....

....

Draw a picture of your favourite ride.

2. How could you make your favourite ride better? Write some sentences saying what would happen if you made it magical!

....

....

....

....

....

The Magic Tree

Hello children. It's time for our Learning To Listen story.
Lie down with your back on the mat or lean forward and put your head on your table.
Make sure you're not touching anyone. Close your eyes. Remember we are learning to actively listen for a sustained amount of time.
Now take a deep breath, hold it, and let it out slowly. Do it again, breathe in ... and out. Breathe in, and out. I want you to keep taking deep breaths while I read you a story.

Listen carefully.

Today you are going for a walk in the forest. You're following the track as it winds its way through the trees. It's a lovely warm day, and you can hear birds singing in the trees. There are many kinds of trees around you; tall trees with thick trunks that reach to the sky, small bushy shrubs covered with tiny flowers, and tiny mosses growing on the ground beneath them. You enjoy the calmness of being in the green forest.

But suddenly you stop walking. Right in front of you is the strangest tree you ever saw! It is a big tree with long branches that reach out towards you. And the funniest thing about it is, the tree is not green, but blue! A blue tree! You have never seen a blue tree before! The leaves are blue, the branches are blue, and the trunk is blue. What a funny tree.

You walk closer to it and look up. The blue tree is so tall you cannot see the top of it! You walk up to the trunk. The branches are spiralling out from the tree trunk, almost like a spiral staircase. It looks like you can climb up into the tree. You put your foot on the bottom branch and step up onto it. The branch seems very strong. You take another step up, then another. When you have climbed five branches, you stop. There are some strange things hanging from the branches here. They look like bananas, but instead of being yellow, they are pink! Pink bananas? You pick one, and open it. The banana is pink inside too. You have a taste, and it tastes just like a real banana. Mmmm. That was delicious.

It's time to keep climbing. Up, up, up you climb in the magic tree. When you have climbed five more branches, you stop.

There are some strange things hanging from the branches here. They look like apples, but instead of being red or green, they are purple! Purple apples? You pick one, and bite into it. It is purple on the inside too, but it tastes just like a real apple. Mmmm. That was delicious.

It's time to keep climbing. Up, up, up you climb in the magic tree. When you have climbed five branches, you stop. There are some strange things hanging from the branches here. They look like oranges, but instead of being orange, they are black. Black oranges? You pick one, and peel off some of the skin. The orange is black inside too. You have a taste, and it tastes just like a real orange! Mmmm. That was delicious.

You look up now, and you're so surprised to find that you have come to the top of tree. You sit up in the top of the blue tree, enjoying the view. But suddenly there is a lot of noise! There is whistling and chirping and singing! The birds have come to the magic blue tree! You sit and watch in amazement as hundreds of birds of all kinds come to eat the fruit from the magic tree. They each take one of the pink bananas or the purple apples or the black oranges. Then they all fly away again with a flutter of wings. Wow! That was great to watch.

It's time to go now. Carefully and slowly you climb back down the branches. Past the black oranges, past the purple apples, and past the pink bananas. Then your feet are back on the ground again. It's time to go home. You hope another day you will see the magic blue tree again!

We're going to take three deep breaths again. Breathe in, hold, and slowly breathe out. Then again, breathe in, and out. Breathe in, and out.
Good. Now slowly sit up.
We've finished.
Well done.

The Magic Tree

Listening Comprehension

1. **Put a circle around the fruit that you saw growing on the magic tree. Colour each the colour they were in the magic tree.**

2. **Choose a word from the list below to fill in the sentence.**

apples	birds	forest	bananas	blue	oranges

   a) You are going for a walk in the ....

   b) You see a tree which is ....

   c) You see pink ....

   d) You see purple ....

   e) You see black ....

   f) The fruit is eaten by the ....

3. **Draw a picture of the magic tree.**

The Magic Tree

Creative Expression

1. **Imagine you find your own magic tree.**

   What would it look like? ....

   ....

   ....

   What would be growing on it? ....

   ....

   ....

   ....

   In the story, birds came and ate all the fruit. Who would come to eat the fruit on your tree?

   ....

   ....

   ....

   ....

2. **Imagine that something different grew on the tree. What about an ice cream tree? Or a pizza tree? Write a list of all the strange and wonderful magic trees you could have!**

   ....

   ....

   ....

   ....

   ....

3. **Draw a forest of magic trees.**

The New Playground

Hello children. It's time for our Learning To Listen story.
Lie down with your back on the mat or lean forward and put your head on your table.
Make sure you're not touching anyone. Close your eyes. Remember we are learning to actively listen for a sustained amount of time.
Now take a deep breath, hold it, and let it out slowly. Do it again, breathe in ... and out. Breathe in, and out. I want you to keep taking deep breaths while I read you a story.

Listen carefully.

Today you're going to the new playground. Yesterday there were workers there, taking away the old swings and slides and the new playground is going to be ready to play on today!
You can't wait to see what exciting things there will be to see and do.
Now you're here, and what a sight! You don't know where to look first! There are two red curvy slides, three green swings, a wobbly bridge, and a flying fox! There is a brown climbing wall, and purple monkey bars to swing on.
The first things you want to try are the red slides. You climb up the ladder, and onto the top of the slide. Wow! You are so high that you can see all over the park. You sit down on the slide, and push off. Whoosh! Down the slide you fly, your body rocking from side to side as you whiz around the corners. Then your feet are on the ground again, and you realise that you're at the bottom of the slide! You'd really like to have another turn, but then you see something else. The swings!
You run over to a green swing and sit on the seat. You put the safety chain around your waist and then you're swinging your legs. Back and forth, back and forth. And you're slowly starting to move! You keep bringing your legs up and down until you're going higher and higher. This is so much fun! The wind blows through your hair as you swing. You stop swinging, and finally your legs touch the ground again. You'd really like to have another turn, but then you see something else. The wobbly bridge!
You climb up onto the wobbly bridge. It is made of slats of wood, held together by chains. You step onto it, and it moves! Every time you take a step, the bridge wobbles everywhere! Step-by-step you walk across the bridge, and then suddenly you're on the other side. You'd really like to have another turn, but then you see something else. The flying fox!
You stand up on the platform, and reach out for the handle. Holding on tightly, you swing your body back, and then with a rush you leap forward. You're flying through the air!
Swish! Suddenly your feet are touching the platform on the other side. You'd really like to have another turn, but then you see something else. The climbing wall!
You walk to the bottom of the brown wall and look up. It does look high! You put your hands into the holes in the wall, and pull yourself up. Then you put your feet into the holes at the bottom. Now where should you put your hands? Up there? Yes. You stretch up as far as you can, and then your feet are coming up too. Up with your hands, up with your feet. Up, up, up. And then you're at the top of the wall! You'd really like to have another turn, but then you see something else. The monkey bars!
You walk over to the purple monkey bars, and reaching out with both hands, you jump up onto the bars. Then you start to swing your body back and forth, and then just as you come forward, you reach out for the next bar. And then the next. You're doing it! You're swinging across the bars like a monkey! Then you're at the end. You'd really like to have another turn, but it's time to go home. Never mind. You can come back another day. What a great playground!

We're going to take three deep breaths again. Breathe in, hold, and slowly breathe out. Then again, breathe in, and out. Breathe in, and out.
Good. Now slowly sit up.
We've finished.
Well done.

The New Playground

Listening Comprehension

1. **Draw a line to match the pieces of the playground with the correct description.**

   a) The slides are   green

   b) The bridge is   red and curvy

   c) The swings are   brown

   d) The monkey bars are   purple

   e) The climbing wall is   made of wood

2. **Write a sentence saying how to use the following playground items:**

   The slide – ....

   ....

   ....

   The flying fox – ....

   ....

   ....

   The climbing wall – ....

   ....

   ....

3. **Draw a map of the playground in the story. Include – the slides, the swings, the bridge, the climbing wall, the flying fox and the monkey bars.**

The New Playground

Creative Expression

1. **What is your favourite part of the playground? Complete the sentences.**

   My favourite thing is ....

   ....

   The reason I like it is ....

   ....

   ....

   The first time I went on it I felt ....

   ....

   ....

2. **Imagine that you are going to design your very own playground. List 10 things you would want to include.**

   1 – ....   2 – ....

   3 – ....   4 – ....

   5 – ....   6 – ....

   7 – ....   8 – ....

   9 – ....   10 – ....

3. **Draw a map of your playground. Colour it in.**

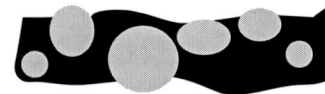

The Pet Store

Hello children. It's time for our Learning To Listen story.
Lie down with your back on the mat or lean forward and put your head on your table.
Make sure you're not touching anyone. Close your eyes. Remember we are learning to actively listen for a sustained amount of time.
Now take a deep breath, hold it, and let it out slowly. Do it again, breathe in ... and out. Breathe in, and out. I want you to keep taking deep breaths while I read you a story.

Listen carefully.

Today we are going to visit the pet shop. You are very happy because you are allowed to choose a pet to take home. You can't wait to find the animal that is going to be your new friend.

You have arrived at the pet shop. When you push open the door, you hear so many sounds! It is very noisy at the front of the pet shop, so you walk down to the back. Here there are a lot of fish swimming around in tanks.

There are so many fish, and they are all beautiful colours. You see orange fish with long floaty tails and black fish with googly eyes. There are big fish and tiny fish. Some are pretty to look at, and some are scary.

Is a fish going to be your new pet? Maybe. But then you see something else.

It's in a glass tank too. You look in, and see a green shell, four legs and a long neck. It's a turtle! The turtle is swimming around in his tank. His long neck moves in and out of his shell, and he looks like he has a smile on his face. You watch him as he climbs out of the water, and onto a rock.

Is a turtle going to be your new pet? Maybe. But then you see something else.

It's another animal in a tank. You look in and see some strange creatures! They are small and wriggly and black. Some have tails, and some have little legs. They are tadpoles! You can also see some small frogs sitting on the rocks. As you watch, one of them flicks out a long tongue and catches a fly! Wow! That was so fast; you can't believe your eyes.

Is a frog going to be your new pet? Maybe. But then you see something else.

There is a big cage, with black and white balls of fluff in them. What can they be? Then you notice that each ball of fluff has two long ears. They are three rabbits! As you watch they hop about their cage, nibbling on carrots. Their noses twitch, and their whiskers quiver as you watch them. They are very cute.

Is a rabbit going to be your new pet? Maybe. But then you hear something else.

It's coming from the bird cages! The birds are making a lot of noise. Some are singing pretty tunes, while others are squawking loudly. There are yellow canaries, blue and purple budgies, and red and green parrots. Some of them are shy, and hide their heads under their wings. Some of them are friendly, and they talk to you, saying "pretty boy".

Is a bird going to be your new pet? Maybe. But then you see something else.

It's a big cage full of puppies! When you count them, you can see there are five in the cage. They are rolling around the cage as they play together. When they see you they stop playing, and come over to you. You look at their silky coats and their big brown eyes. Is a puppy going to be your new pet? Yes! This is the animal you want to be your new pet. The pet shop owner comes over and asks you which puppy you would like. You choose a white one, with a brown patch over his eye. The pet shop owner picks him up and puts him in your hand. He is so soft and warm!

What a great friend this little puppy is going to be!

We're going to take three deep breaths again. Breathe in, hold, and slowly breathe out. Then again, breathe in, and out. Breathe in, and out.
Good. Now slowly sit up.
We've finished.
Well done.

The Pet Store

Listening Comprehension

1. **Make a list of all the pets you saw in the pet shop and what they were kept in. (The first letter has been done for you.)**

   f..............   kept in ....

   b..............   kept in ....

   r..............   kept in ....

   t..............   kept in ....

   f.............. and t..............   kept in ....

   p..............   kept in ....

2. **Draw a line to match the pet with the correct description.**

   a) puppy   long floaty tails

   b) fish   small and wriggly

   c) turtle   big brown eyes

   d) rabbit   long neck

   e) tadpole   singing songs

   f) bird   two long ears

3. **Draw a picture of the pet that was chosen.**

4. **Put the animals next to the correct number.**

   many – ....

              ....

   3 – ....

   5 – ....

   1 – ....

Creative Expression

1. Draw a circle around the things you might see in a pet shop. Colour them in.

2. What animals do you like to see when you visit the pet shop? Write a list of all the pets you can think of.

....

....

....

....

3. What animal would make an unusual pet? Maybe an elephant, or a giraffe! Write some sentences saying how you would look after your strange pet!

Animal name:...

....

Where would you keep it?...

....

What would you feed it?...

....

Where would you play with it? ....

....

The Storm

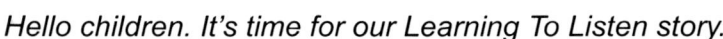

Hello children. It's time for our Learning To Listen story.
Lie down with your back on the mat or lean forward and put your head on your table.
Make sure you're not touching anyone. Close your eyes. Remember we are learning to actively listen for a sustained amount of time.
Now take a deep breath, hold it, and let it out slowly. Do it again, breathe in ... and out. Breathe in, and out. I want you to keep taking deep breaths while I read you a story.

Listen carefully.

Today you are going for a walk. You leave your house, and walk down the street, in the direction of the beach. After about 20 minutes walking, you arrive at the beach. You sit down on a park bench to catch your breath. As you sit you notice the big clouds on the horizon. Big, purple clouds, and they're moving fast! The wind is picking up, and it's blowing straight off the sea. And it's bringing the big purple clouds towards you!

You think it's time to head home. As you walk, you keep an eye on the big purple clouds. They are quite close now. Their colours are quite amazing; they are so dark, they have turned grey. A deep dark grey. You walk a little closer, and then you see a rain drop fall on the ground in front of you. Then another, and another! Big round raindrops are dropping on your head and on your face! You walk as fast as you can, but you know you're not going to be home before the rain comes. Just as the raindrops start falling, you see a big tree in front of you. The branches of the tree stretch out over the footpath. This would be a good place to shelter until the shower is over. You run under the tree, and just in time. Down comes the rain! Raindrops are falling everywhere around you, but it's quite dry under the tree. You can smell an earthy scent as the rain soaks into the ground and into the trees and plants around you. You can hear the pitter-patter of the rain on the ground, and the drip, drip, drip of the raindrops falling from the branches.

After a while you notice that the rain has lessened. You poke your head out from under the branches and look around. The storm cloud has gone. But there is another one coming! And it's bigger and blacker than the last one! Will you have time to get home? You start to run as fast as you can! Down the road, around the corner and then you can see your house. Just as you reach your driveway, it starts to rain again. You dash up the drive, and open the front door and step inside. As you close your door, it starts to pour! The rain pours down on your roof, and it is so loud that it sounds like a roar. You rush to the window and look out. And then you see what is making such a loud noise. It is hailing! Little balls of ice are falling from the sky and bouncing all over the driveway. Soon the ground is covered in white hail.

Suddenly you see a bright flash across the sky. It's lightning! Wow! It was shaped like a huge fork across the sky. You look to see if there is any more lightning, but then you hear a huge rumble right above your house. It is thunder! What a loud crashing sound it makes! As you watch there is another flash of lightning, and then another clap of thunder. But it wasn't quite as loud as the first one. There are more lightning flashes, and more thunderclaps, but they are getting further away. The storm is moving away now.

Finally, it stops raining. You open your door, and step outside. Wow! The ground is still covered in hail. It looks like it has been snowing! But as you watch, the sun comes out from behind the clouds, and the hail begins to melt.

The storm has gone. What an amazing storm it was!

We're going to take three deep breaths again. Breathe in, hold, and slowly breathe out. Then again, breathe in, and out. Breathe in, and out.
Good. Now slowly sit up.
We've finished.
Well done.

The Storm

Listening Comprehension

1. Draw a line to match the names in List A to the descriptions in List B.

A	B
Clouds	A huge rumbling sound
Raindrops	A huge fork in the sky
Hail	It looks like snow
Thunder	Dropping on your head
Lightning	Big and purple

2. Draw a picture of yourself sheltering under a big tree with long overhanging branches. It is raining. Label the following parts on your picture:

– the cloud   – the raindrops   – the big tree   – the long branches

3. Answer these questions about the story.

a) What did you hear? ....

....

b) What did you see? ....

....

c) What did you smell? ....

....

The Storm

Creative Expression

1. **Think about the sounds that a storm makes. List all the noisy words you can think of to describe a storm.**

   a) Rain sounds . ...

   ....

   b) Wind sounds . ...

   ....

   c) Hail sounds . ...

   ....

   d) Thunder sounds. ....

   ....

2. **Draw a picture of your favourite part of a storm. Put yourself in the picture, watching from a safe place inside.**

3. **Write a paragraph about a time when you got caught in the rain.**

   ....

   ....

   ....

   ....

   ....

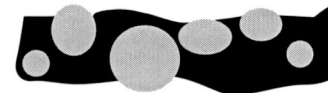

Hello children. It's time for our Learning To Listen story.
Lie down with your back on the mat or lean forward and put your head on your table.
Make sure you're not touching anyone. Close your eyes. Remember we are learning to actively
listen for a sustained amount of time.
Now take a deep breath, hold it, and let it out slowly. Do it again, breathe in ... and out. Breathe in, and
out. I want you to keep taking deep breaths while I read you a story.

Listen carefully.

Today you are going shopping. As you walk along the street, you see many shops. There is a hardware shop, a bakery, and a flower shop. Suddenly you stop. You are standing outside a shop that you have never seen before. It has an old red door, with cobwebs all over it. The writing on the window says, "Hobgoblin Wizardry Supplies". The window is very dusty and you can't see into the shop. So you push open the door, and step inside.

There is a long counter along the side of the shop. Behind it are shelves full of coloured glass bottles. And in the glass bottles are the most amazing powders. They are brightly coloured, from reds, pinks and purples, to greens, blues and yellows.

Just then, a wizard comes out from behind a curtain. He is tall and thin, and he is wearing a long pointed hat, covered in stars. His body is covered by a dark blue cloak that sweeps to the ground. "Can I help you?" he asks in a friendly voice. "No thank you, I'm just looking," you say. The door opens and a short wizard enters the shop. He is also wearing a long pointed hat, and he wears a purple cloak.

"Hello," he says to the tall wizard. "I would like to buy a spell to make my ears grow as a long as a rabbit's."

"Certainly," says the tall wizard. You watch in amazement as the tall wizard takes an empty jar from under the counter. He takes one pinch of red powder, two pcms of blue powder, and three pinches of yellow powder, puts them in the jar, and stirs them with his wand. He waves the wand over the colourful jar. "Hoppity, loppity hoe, rabbit ears you will grow," he says. He gives the jar to the short wizard, who gives him five pieces of gold money. Then the short wizard leaves the shop.

In comes a witch. She is wearing a long black cloak, and black pointed hat. "Good morning," she says to the tall wizard. "I would like to buy a spell that will make my broomstick faster."

"Certainly," says the tall wizard. The tall wizard takes an empty jar from under the counter. He takes one pinch of purple powder and two pinches of yellow powder; he puts them in the jar, and stirs them with his wand. He waves the wand over the colourful jar. "Lister, loster, laster, make this broomstick faster," he says. He gives the jar to the witch, who gives him five pieces of gold money. Then the witch leaves the store.

In comes an elf. He is wearing a green suit that fits his tiny frame tightly. "Good morning," he says to the tall wizard. "I would like to buy a spell that will turn carrots blue."

"Certainly," says the tall wizard. The tall wizard takes an empty jar from under the counter. He takes one pinch of orange powder and three pinches of black powder, puts them in the jar, and stirs them with his wand. He waves the wand over the colourful jar. "Knicky, knacky knoo, turn your carrots blue," he says. He gives the jar to the elf, who gives him five pieces of gold money. Then the elf leaves the shop.

It is time for you to go now too.

"Goodbye," says the tall wizard. "Come back another time."

"Goodbye," you say as you walk out of the shop. You would like to go back there another time. What a strange and wonderful wizard's shop!

We're going to take three deep breaths again. Breathe in, hold, and slowly breathe out. Then again,
breathe in, and out. Breathe in, and out.
Good. Now slowly sit up.
We've finished.
Well done.

The Wizard's Store

Listening Comprehension

1. Here are some sentences from the story. Put a circle around the correct answer.

   a) The shop has a new/old door.

   b) There is a long/short counter in the shop.

   c) The wizard is wearing a cloak covered with stars/moons.

   d) The witch wants a spell to make her broomstick faster/slower.

   e) The elf wants to turn his carrots blue/purple.

2. Three customers came into the shop. What were they wearing? Draw a line to match the descriptions to the correct customer.

   a) The short wizard   Green suit

   b) The witch   Purple cloak, long pointed hat.

   c) The elf   Long black cloak, black pointed hat.

3. Draw a picture of the three customers.

the short wizard

the witch

the elf

The Wizard's Store

Creative Expression

1. **Just suppose you did buy a spell from the tall wizard.**

   What spell would you get? ....

   ....

   What colour powders would the wizard use to make your spell? ....

   ....

   What magic words would the wizard say to make your spell work? ....

   ....

   ....

   ....

   How many gold pieces would you pay for your spell? ....

2. **Design a hat and a cloak for a witch or wizard. Write a sentence about what they would look like.**

   The hat would be ....

   ....

   The cloak would be ....

   ....

3. **Draw a picture of a witch or wizard wearing your hat and cloak.**

Visiting The Circus

Hello children. It's time for our Learning To Listen story.
Lie down with your back on the mat or lean forward and put your head on your table.
Make sure you're not touching anyone. Close your eyes. Remember we are learning to actively listen for a sustained amount of time.
Now take a deep breath, hold it, and let it out slowly. Do it again, breathe in ... and out. Breathe in, and out. I want you to keep taking deep breaths while I read you a story.

Listen carefully.

Today you are going to visit the circus! You are so excited because you haven't been to a circus before. What wonderful things will you see? The show you are going to see is at night, and you have to wait all day. Then you dress in your best clothes and off you go!

When you arrive at the circus, you see a gigantic red tent, lit up by bright lights. The sign says, 'Welcome to the Big Top!' That must be the name for the tent. You line up at the ticket booth to get your ticket. Then you give the woman your money, and you're in the circus area!

You hear a voice coming from a speaker nearby, "Please take your seats! The show is about to begin."

You find the opening in the Big Top and you go in. What a wonderful sight! The Big Top is huge! There are seats all the way around, and you find yours, which luckily is right at the front.

Then the lights go out! It's very dark, but then a spotlight comes on, and out comes the Ringmaster. He is wearing a black suit, a black top hat, and a black cloak. "Ladies and Gentlemen! Welcome to the Big Top! Your first act is the tightrope walker, Marmaduke Muddles!" The curtain opens and out comes a very small man. He is wearing a tight-fitting suit of sparkling silver. He takes a bow, and then he turns and climbs up a very thin ladder. He stops, turns to the centre of the ring, and takes a skinny pole from beside the ladder. What is he going to do? Then you see! There is a tiny stretch of wire running across the middle of the Big Top. Is Marmaduke Muddles going to walk on it? It looks impossible! But then, very slowly Marmaduke Muddles steps onto the wire. He balances his pole in front of him, and step-by-step, he walks across the stretch of wire! The crowd is so quiet, but as soon as he is across to the other side, they burst out clapping! Marmaduke Muddles climbs down the ladder, and gives a big bow. Then he has gone.

Then the Ringmaster says, "Here she comes the amazing, Juggling Jane!" Out comes a woman dressed in a suit of sparkling blue. She bows to the crowd, and points to her assistant, who hands her three brightly coloured balls. She throws them high in the air, and as they fall down she quickly catches them again, and up they go! Around and around. Then her assistant hands her two more balls. Up they go too! Now she is juggling five balls! And then two more! Up they go, and now she is juggling seven balls! They are just colourful blurs, and you're felling quite dizzy from watching them going around and around! All at once Juggling Jane stops and does a big bow. Everyone claps and cheers as she leaves the stage.

The Ringmaster comes out again. "Ladies and Gentlemen, we have time for one more act. It's Lulu the dancing dog!" Everyone claps as a big white poodle runs into the ring. Even Lulu is wearing a tiny red hat on her head! As the music starts, Lulu stands up on her back legs, and starts to dance! She is barking and dancing in time with the music! Then she stops, and everyone claps.

"Thank you," says the Ringmaster. "Please come back and see our show again."

We're going to take three deep breaths again. Breathe in, hold, and slowly breathe out. Then again, breathe in, and out. Breathe in, and out.
Good. Now slowly sit up.
We've finished.
Well done.

Visiting The Circus

Listening Comprehension

1. Here are some statements from the story. Choose an answer from the list to finish the sentence.

hat	Big Top	seven	front	tight rope	black

a) The name of the tent is the ....

b) Your seat is at the ....

c) The ringmaster is wearing a .... suit.

d) Marmaduke Muddles walks on the ....

e) Juggling Jane can juggle .... balls.

f) Lulu is wearing a tiny red ....

2. Write some sentences to describe how:

Marmaduke Muddles walks on the tightrope – ....

....

....

Juggling Jane juggles her seven balls – ....

....

....

Lulu the poodle dances – ....

....

....

3. Draw a picture of your favourite circus performer.

Visiting The Circus

Creative Expression

1. **What other circus acts might you see at a circus? Make a list of your ideas.**

   ....

   ....

   ....

   ....

   ....

   ....

2. **Choose your favourite circus act from the list. Write some sentences on how to do it.**

   My favourite circus act is ....

   How is it done? ....

   ....

   ....

   ....

   ....

   ....

   ....

3. **Draw a picture of your favourite circus act.**

A Visit To The Fire Station – page 2
1. Circles around – boots, helmet, fire fighter's pants, fire fighter's jacket.
2. a – False, b – True, c- True, d – False, e – True, f – False.

Dinosaur Dig – page 5
1. a – True, b – False, c – True, d – False, e – False, f – True.
2. a – An enormous tree, b – 30 paces, c – cloth, d – fallen logs, e – small brush, f – torch.

Feeding Time At The Zoo – page 8
1. a – green, b – blue, c – green, d – yellow, e – red.
2. a – True, b – False, c – False, d – False, e – True.

Fireworks Night – page 11
1. 1 – c, 2 – d, 3 – a, 4 – b.
2. 1st – sky rockets, 2nd – sparkling rain, 3rd – Catherine Wheel, 4th – sparklers.

I Am A Bird – page 14
1. a – True, b – False, c – False, d – False, e – True, f – False, g – False, h – True.
2. a – mark correct either: dark, quiet, warm, cramped. b – mark correct either: hungry, warm, happy. c – mark correct: scared, d – mark correct: Happy, pleased.

I'm A Giant! – page 17
1. a – True, b – False, c – False, d – False, e – False, f – True.
2. a – dream, b – waves, c – cows, d – steps, e – colder.

Rainbow Ride – page 20
1. Red, orange, yellow, green, blue, indigo, violet.
2. Mark correct:
   R – fire, sunset, rubies, roses, tomatoes
   O – sunrise, carrots, pumpkins, peaches, apricots
   Y – sunlight, daffodils, butter, canaries
   G – forest, emerald, sage, jade, trees
   B – ocean, sky
   I – royalty, grapes, eggplants
   V – lavender, pansy, lilac.
3. a – False, b – True, c – True, d – False.

Riding The Steam Train – page 23
1. a – you don't miss the train, b – before you see it, c – into the station, d – the back carriage, e – clips your ticket, f – go passed the cars, g – coal and smoke.
2. a – All Aboard, b – Tickets please, c – Clackety clack, d – toot toot, e – hissssssssss.
3. b, d, a, c.

Seaside Walk – page 26
1. Circles around – shell, fish, pebbles, seagull, seaweed, crab.
2. Mark correct either: Seagulls – squawking, flapping, Waves – suck, slap.
3. Seaweed, fish, crab.

The Dolls' House – page 29
1. Circles around – doll house, garden tools, bicycle, painting.
2. a – wood, b – tiles, c – leafy vine, d – staircase, e – white bath, f – wallpaper.

The Fairy Ring – page 32
1. a – False, b – True, c – False, d – False, e – True, f – False, g – True.
2. a – yellow leaves, b – forest, c – toadstools, d – rainbow, e – vests, f – gold, g – white, h – tallest finger.

The Gingerbread Cottage – page 35
1. a – The right track, b – a gingerbread cottage, c – a chocolate button, d – behind the curtains, e – a witch, f – the cat's whiskers, g – a sore throat.
2. Circles around – 4-leaf clover, 4 flowers, cat's whiskers, whistle.
3. a – golden, b – pink and blue, c – brown, d – black, e – green, f – blue.

The Kite – page 38
1. 1st – c, 2nd – b, 3rd – f, 4th – a, 5th – d, 6th – e.
2. Picture.
3. a – No, b – Power lines, c – No, d – School.

The Magic Carousel – page 41
1. Circle around – Ferris wheel, carousal horse, stars, roller coaster.
2. You can smell hot dogs and candyfloss. Two other rides are the roller coaster and the slide. The carousal is gold and red. Your horse is purple, gold and red. Your horse jumps off the carousel. You feel as if you could touch the stars. It is getting cold and you shiver. You climb off your horse and thank him for the ride.
3. a – yes, b – no, c – no, d – no, e – yes, f – no, g – no, h – yes.

The Magic Tree – page 44
1. Circle around – apple, banana, orange.
2. Bananas – pink, apples – purple, oranges – black.
3. a – forest, b – blue, c – bananas, d – apples, e – oranges, f – birds.

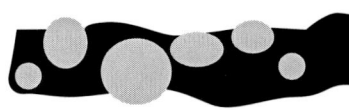

The New Playground – page 47

1. a – red and curvy, b – made of wood, c – green,
   d – purple, e – brown.
2. The slide – sit down on the slide and push off.
   The flying fox – reach for the handle, hold on
   tight, swing back, leap forward.
   The climbing wall – put your hands and feet in
   the holes. Reach up and pull yourself up.

The Pet Shop – page 50

1. Fish – tank, Birds – cage, Rabbits – cage, Turtles
   – tank, Frogs and tadpoles – tank,
   Puppies – cage.
2. a) Puppy – big brown eyes, b) fish – long floaty
   tails, c) turtle – long neck, d) rabbit – two
   long ears, e) tadpole – small and wriggly,
   f) bird – singing songs.
4. Many – fish, birds, frogs and tadpoles,
   3 – rabbits, 5 – puppies, 1 – turtle.

The Storm – page 53

1. Clouds – big and purple. Raindrops – dropping
   on your head. Hail – it looks like snow.
   Thunder – a huge rumbling sound.
   Lightning – a huge fork in the sky.
2. Mark correct if the child has labelled accurately
   – cloud, raindrops, big tree, long branches.
3. a – pitter-patter, dripping of the rain. Hail
   falling on the roof. Rumble of thunder.
   b – clouds, rain, hail, lightning, sun. c – an
   earthy smell.

The Wizard's Shop – page 56

1. a – old, b – long, c – stars, d – faster, e – blue.
2. a – purple cloak, long pointed hat. b – long
   black cloak, black pointed hat. c – green suit.

Visiting The Circus – page 59

1. a – Big Top, b – front, c – black, d – tightrope,
   e – seven, f – hat.
2. Marmaduke Muddles – climbs up the thin
   ladder. He takes a pole and then walks slowly
   across the wire, holding the pole in front of him.
   He gets to the other side and climbs down.
   Juggling Jane – She throws three balls high in
   the air, then she juggles five balls, and then she
   juggles seven balls.
   Lulu the poodle – She stands on her back legs
   and dances to the music.